ADANNA
LITERARY JOURNAL

How Women Grieve

Founder
CHRISTINE REDMAN-WALDEYER

Guest Editor
LYNNE MCENIRY

Adanna accepts poetry, fiction, essays, and book reviews. Please send a proposal for reviews. All submissions are electronically accepted in one file, preferably a word document file with a cover letter and a three to four line bio.

Visit our website for further details:
www.adannajournal.blogspot.com

Adanna Literary Journal
P.O. Box 547
Manasquan, New Jersey 08736 USA

ISBN: 978-0-9836463-3-4

Credits

Cover Art: Elizabeth Catanese
Cover Title: River

Back Cover: Maurice Thomassen
Cover Title: Color Blind

Cover Design: David Crews

Copyright © 2012. All rights reserved by *Adanna Literary Journal.*

Artists' Statement

My work explores the signs and symbols humans make to represent experience. More specifically, it explores the semiotics of history and the signs and symbols I have used to navigate aspects of my personal history: the losses and longings in my life thus far. In addition to using physical objects in my work, I am also interested in words as objects. When I paint, I negotiate the chasm between the non-verbal (shapes, line, color, and form) and the constant stream of text running through my brain that I often cannot turn off. I use mortar on my canvases because in the world of masonry, mortar serves the utilitarian function of closing the gaps between building materials like brick and stone in the same way that the signs and symbols humans use are attempts to close the gaps, the difficult or hard to name experiences, in our lives.

I began *River* by placing mortar in the center of the canvas and writing "this is the place where words wash away." Next, I spelled words with their letters out of order. I filled in the rest of the image with thinned blue, black and gray acrylic paint to represent water and included glitter to replicate the sun's reflection on the water. In this piece, I am playing with the idea that words can be as permanent as cement and as mobile as water in a river. They are a force of solidity that captures the human experience and a force of life moving through the world.

Elizabeth Catanese
– *River*

Artists' Statement

In my work, I challenge the borders of painting by combining innovative and traditional materials and techniques. I paint, for example, with coffee, sillicone paste, tempera, acrylics, oil paints and veneer. I glue elements on canvas, print elements beforehand, or wash paints into the unprepared canvas. This way the painting develops step-by-step and results in numerous layers. The beginning point of a painting (series) often lies in newspaper or other media image material, which refer to a current socio-political and/or controversial issue. The original images are often work in contradiction with the related article or reflect only partly (subjectively) the particular news issue. By reconstructing these images with a multi-layered collage technique, I am able to analyse media strategies. Through the whole process the original picture, and thereby the related news issue, is transformed. Therefore, the finished painting reveals (a) different point(s) of view and questions public opinion. The titles connect parallels between different paintings of a whole series. My work as a whole can be seen as series of to-be questioned, implicit and explicit statements, about (im)possibilities of painting, the (absurd) world we live in, and the way images function and communicate today.

Maurice Thomassen
– Color Blind

Adanna's Mission Statement

Adanna, a name of Nigerian origin, pronounced a-DAN-a, is defined as "her father's daughter." I chose to name this literary journal *Adanna* because women over the centuries have been defined by men in politics, through marriage, and most importantly, by the men who fathered them. In college, I was inspired by women such as Anne Hutchinson who had the opportunity to study under her father. Today women are still bound by complex roles in society, often needing to wear more than one hat or sacrifice one role so another may flourish. While this journal is dedicated to women, it is not exclusive, and it welcomes our counterparts and their thoughts about women today. I only ask that your submissions reflect women's issue or topics, celebrate womanhood, or shout out in passion.

Christine Redman-Waldeyer, Founder

Introduction

Jane Hirshfield enters the world of the poem in <u>Nine Gates</u>. Here she finds that poetry can be the vessel of remembrance.

"The story of poetry has many beginnings. One is in Mnemosyne—Remembrance—earliest born of the Greek goddesses, mother of the Muses and so also of the poem. Hesiod calls her the goddess of the first hour, as it would have to be: at the moment that time appears in the world, change appears in the world, and change alone, lacking memory's steadying counterweight would mean Chaos...Through Mnemosyne, the knowable world continues from moment to moment, and through the poetry she engendered, words first learned to transcend time...In Mnemosyne's time, memory was not yet imagined as a book or a storage room into which one could look."

The poet, human, must endure loss and grieve over change. Without Mnemosyne, we could not find that room to store what is most dear to us. If there is a triumph over loss, it is with what we cherish most, memory. Language, words, letters, come together to give form, give body to what is retrieved to make it present. Where can we house our grief other than our hearts, in the very being of soul, and where might we contain it to relieve our spirit of its burden? Memory can help us move on as much as it can help us to remember. In writing out our grief, visiting memory, we can free the flightless bird in that hour.

Jane Hirshfield reminds us that we are the creator of not the space that holds our memory, but what we fill it with. In her poem "The Room" she writes:

A room does not turn its back on grief.
Anger does not excite it.
Before desire, it neither responds
nor draws back in fear.

Without changing expression,
it takes
and gives back;
not a tuft in the mattress alters.

If we are to model ourselves after the room, we can even find the strength to hold on during that grieving period in whatever stage we may move onto or retreat to; it is in that understanding that we can also see ourselves become nothing more.

Whatever disquiet we sense in a room
we have brought there.

And so I instruct my ribs each morning,
pointing to hinge and plaster and wood -

You are matter, as they are.
See how perfectly it can be done.
Hold, one day more, what is asked.
~from The Lives of the Heart (Harper Perrenial, 1997)

Jane Hirshfield writes that "Human vision divides…but a sound is perceived as coming toward and entertaining into us, bringing the outer within: sound lives in the movement of our own inner bones joining the resonance of its prior source…what is heard—the cry of a child—the fall of a cougar's foot in dry leaves—is always the sign of something changing: only something active makes a noise." And indeed grief is active. In poetry, we attempt to reign in what we cannot control, but Jane also implores us to see something magical in sound. It names what is nameless. As she argues, Adam named the animals, so we too name our grief. By calling on memory, we make the past an active part of our present lives. And I too remember, move forward, retreat, remember again. In "Fall" I recollect what was good, what has passed, and what I cannot change.

Fall

I'm asking for one more warm day before winter an Indian summer day a day like the one I shared with you at the boardwalk on the roller coaster when you were ticketed for urinating in public behind the building in the parking lot where meters ticked away behind the screams of ride goers. Loose change a curfew we stayed out late ate popcorn blue cotton candy that stained our lips laughed later when a bird shattered itself against the motion of the car, caught itself on the wipers. It was you who would be our hero removing it from our vision. If only I had returned your call one week earlier, I would have seen you fly once more.

Christine Redman-Waldeyer

Contents

Introduction
Christine Redman-Waldeyer

POETRY

13	Jasmine Araujo	45	Adele Kenny
14	Cara Armstrong	46	Patricia Kinney
15	Wendy Barnes	47	Alyse Knorr
17	Elliott batTzedek	49	Judy Kronenfeld
19	Christine Beck	51	Michelle Lerner
21	Mary Brancaccio	52	Kristin Leskowits
23	Elizabeth Catanese	53	Antoinette Libro
24	Luisa Caycedo-Kimura	54	Charlotte Mandel
26	Lucia Cherciu	55	Yesenia Montilla
27	Barbara Crooker	57	Pat Mottola
28	Jessica G. de Koninck	59	Megeen R. Mulholland
31	Kathy Engel	62	Michelle Ovalle
32	Anna M. Evans	63	Linda Radice
33	Meri Harary Fleischman	65	Mina Santomenno
34	Marisa Frasca	66	Heidi Sheridan
36	Celeste Gainey	67	Lisa Sisler
37	Roberto Carlos Garcia	68	Odarka Polanskyj Stockert
38	Deborah Gerrish	70	Anique Taylor
40	Gail Fishman Gerwin	71	Madeline Tiger
42	Sarah Ghoshal	73	Laura Whalen
43	Yueh Goffin	74	Laura Winters
44	M.J. Iuppa		

ESSAY

77	Lynne McEniry
81	Laura Winters

POETRY

Jasmine Araujo

The Dead Make Their Way

My brothers and I use to play in the hulks of broken Leopard
Tanks abandoned in Basrah
Where puffs of uranium dust rose into the ducts of our lungs,
though we sweetly remember.

As we lie in positions that keep us from feeling our dying
Even my mothers clement voice petitioning Allah beside my
bed,

Even that leaves
Because the dark has no will

Only a stillness that stretches into stillness
To which the dead make their way.

Cara Armstrong

Traveling Memories
               (For Ans Hey, Dutch Sculptor, 1932 – 2011)

Farewell to the windows of Amsterdam,
now that your body has been carried over
one of its 379-year-old window sills,

on the way to burial. Brain artery ruptured,
you've left to play in the Marquis de Sade's quarry,
carving wind and tables of love in Lacoste.

Your final words trickled out
in English--
       Love is Fantastic--

capturing the taste of Appalachia's mired spring,
Key West's flamboyanas knocking our eyes out,
the Singel Canal's pushcart herrings.

We touched the Ashkenazi synagogue's stone
where you left notes to your brother, anyone, all—
letting us know, you survived the war.

              How will he know you're gone?

Wendy Barnes

The Minotaur's Mother

I want you made of planets,
rage, and fire.

The first part of the sentence
is the terror house,

swarming with teeth,
you slipping from me like a rope.

If you say omen or guilt,
if the story says salt,
then salt, then afterburn.

Then in the second part
we are forever tied

in this riddle
of earth and flesh and stone,
voices ravening the air.

I look and look into your face
but cannot find you.

What if, twice, our fate
is thicker than we thought?

If the sky lies once,
it lies again. Far off something laughs
or dies.

Say it's something that I did,
some abscessed promise.
Say something you can't say,

one barren blood. Say "harrow."

Tell me what you are.

Elliott batTzedek

I heard "pulse ox" and then "coding" and then

Timelessness
no   a lack of time and then
all tubed-up in a bed with a view
of Santa Catalina a place where no one
loved me so I lay alone down to
107 pounds so close to my goal
of not being
trays of hospital fare untouched, hunger
just another part of a body
I no longer felt.

As I had not felt myself not breathing, steroids
for the asthma in the distant past
of September's size 16.

On the overnight shift, the one reserved
for gay nurses, fat nurses, old nurses, he
found me awake and shaking, refused to measure
vital signs on someone clearly not but asked
if I would like my back rubbed, skin
no one had touched all the months Orange County
had been digesting me.

Lotion warmed his palms spread wide and
venturesome as God's hands shaping clay pushing
flesh while seeking life spark, he hummed only
soft syllables until I fell asleep enough to wake
to the morning on which I ate.

I could find him, say *thank you*, the gay gossip network
that would be more powerful than the 26 years
slipped past if not for this
hard fact:

it was 1985 in Southern California—

all my sources are on the AIDs quilt
which is itself out of style
and packed away.

Christine Beck

Given Salt, Given Time

I.

Before I knew that olives grew in Spain,
and bloomed on ancient trees, their
accent on the tongue of foreign zest—
Kalamátas, Arbequiñas, Manzañillas,

Before I knew that olives should grow full,
turn black or purple-brown on branches first,
then cured in brine for weeks in wooden casks
their bitter taste stripped out by salt and time,

I thought black olives came in cans called *Ripe*,
displayed on crystal plates in Large or Jumbo size,
unaware they'd been picked green, then dunked
in lye and gassed to turn them black and firm.

II.

Before I knew what burrowed in her skin
would claim my mother's life at fifty-two,
leach out exuberance, her gift of flair,
strip her hair from blonde to driftwood gray,

We holidayed in Spain, slipped into bars,
bought local wine, a meal with cheese and bread,
where *aceitunas,* olives, were required
to turn the commonplace to the sublime.

We feasted on their oily olive skins,
a soft resistance, ooze against the tooth.
With flick of tongue against each fingertip,
we licked the dripping oils and sighed.

III.

That was before I knew what I know now,
that olives on the branch, grown full and lush
will lose their clutch. They fall into the nets
below, still bitter and inedible,

Yet, soaked in brine and stored in casks,
given salt and given time, the olives turn
as delicate as memory, as piquant
as a picnic on a small Majorcan beach.

Mary Brancaccio

Night Watch

Tonight, I squeeze your hand and press rags
to your brow. You ask me for morphine.
After, pain lifts and you drift off. But
now Dad is pissed off, accuses me
of not caring: *Once she's on morphine,
it's all over, she's as good as dead.
How could you do that to your mother?*
Decades ago, I was twelve. You said
(eyes black and matte like polished rocks, voice

low like distant thunder) *I will draw
a knife across my jugular vein.
My blood will paint a liquid necklace.*
For several months, I couldn't sleep.
I'd creep into your room while you slept,
stretch my forefingers toward your nostrils
feeling for exhale of your breath.
Months ago, you climbed Skellig Michael –
woman frail with cancer, fearful of heights.

What prayer pushed you up slick rocky stairs
to the monk's stone hives, clustered above
rough Atlantic waves, where sea birds
wheeled on icy gusts against sharp crags?
What desire for atonement lifted
your footsteps? God, how you loved this earth,
its grit in your teeth, salt on your tongue.
air in your lungs. You conquered old fears --
I leaned…into rock. I watched my feet.

You breathe, you breathe. Short gasps between words.
Tonight, I've no words left. Poor student
that I am, what I want hangs like mist
in your nebulizer, clogs my soles
with street debris gathered from gutters.

Exhalation fogs your mask, emits
hollow sounds of a deep sea diver,
heavy with trill of near-death, livid
pulse of life. Far, far above us, waves.

Elizabeth Catanese

Freezing

My nutritionist says one can freeze
and refreeze
without noticeable difference

in taste,
but in an effort
not to bring you into the poem

I plan to eat the slice
of lemon cake
sitting on this forest green

bedspread
quickly,
gulping custard and cake

'til my stomach hurts.
I plan to throw away all evidence
of the bittersweet,

go to bed full
and alone.

Luisa Caycedo-Kimura

Running Over Broken Glass

She takes an awl, stabs her hand
and feels the neurons flutter
in a conscious stream. A rush

as intense as sex on a public beach.
She's tired of being in her terrarium
while earwigs stare hungrily

as she falls like a seed into sand.
She too is a common earwig
and longs for a damp, dark

crevice, awake to the scent
of warm bark. Ask what it's like to live
in her glass box. She'll tell you

it's like having dung thrown
down her gullet to taste
and inhale. It's pungency burrowing

down to her feet. She tries to find
numbness when it's not there, and screams
in the yard, startling the fireflies. Daily

she must bury a craving to burn
her house down while she sits in it. She alone
knows a caress will cause her to vomit.

A smile will hurt more than flames
or the end of a shovel. When dusk comes
she'll tie up her sneakers and run
until her blood pumps so hard

it covers her pretense. She imagines
she can escape to a forest of skies

—the awl points the way.

Lucia Cherciu

They Drove for Twenty Hours to Clean up the House

Porous, the rooms accumulated
piles from closets to tops of beds,
sheer mix of empty bags, carton boxes,
and one-use gadgets: juicers
with remnants of fruit peel stuck in the blades,
a film of dirt covering the stove and fridge shelves
like jelly. They felt the dead weight
of unwanted gifts, the impulse buys at the dollar store.

Cheap jewelry glittered resigned
like theater props in a treasure trunk:
he didn't have the heart
to throw it out himself, so now the daughters
had to go through it twice. They ordered
a garbage bin and then filled three,
couldn't save the half-dead plants, sticky
with dust. Most fixtures falling apart,
too old to give to Goodwill, shoes
stretched out of shape, folded back
like an accordion.

They tackled letters and diary notebooks:
after reading full pages
about missed deadlines and dentist bills,
they burned them in the backyard.
By the third day they were ready
to paint. In November,
leaves were starting to melt
and rain seeped over clogged gutters.

Barbara Crooker

FIRST SPRING WITHOUT YOU,

Then you'll remember your life / as a book of candles, / each page read by the light of its burning. ("Become Becoming," Li-Young Lee)

and I'm driving south, spring unrolling like a satin ribbon
right off the spool. Trees blur with the whisper of buds,
fresh green hope. You've gone to where there's no coming back
from, and that's the black branched fact. Along the highway,
impossibly purple redbuds arc overhead, and I want to pull
over, take pictures to show you when I return. Time
keeps zigzagging, past/present/past, like that fat red fox
running in the meadow's tall grass. The trees' blossoms
are incandescent as candles, but the Book of Life is fastened
shut, and there are no pages left to read by their own burning.

Jessica G. de Koninck

Common Knots

He looked for the simplest ways to keep
things from falling apart: a screwdriver,
hammer and nails, wrenches,
staplers, glue gun. Taped to the file drawer
directions for various nautical knots.
He would strip down a motor
for hours, then patiently teach
it to hum. Nothing left over
got wasted. He saved wire to make
engines run. Not his own. There's no
happy ending, just glass jars
filled with washers and screws.
Spread them out on the dining
room table. Take whatever
you think you can use.

Jessica G. de Koninck

Salvage

To reverse prolapse
surgeons hold up the bladder
with the skin of a cadaver.

Science stitches up
what gravity pulls down.

Cadaver...

More genteel to say organ transplant
better to say donor. Distasteful
        discussions of corneas, skin, lungs, heart.
        The cash and carry
        business that goes on at night might

get detected. But with casket closed what goes
unnoticed goes unnoticed.
        Picked clean as a car abandoned
        in Camden. Hubcaps,
        headlamps, grill work for sale.

            The business of leftovers,
            like the time we unearthed a steering arm
            and hood latch for the Renault

at a junkyard outside Worcester. Kept
that old hatchback running. So
        at the funeral home I never checked.

I did not ask to look.
With no formaldehyde, wax or makeup,

            a night and a day would only

       make things worse. To the end
your skin remained taut,
        unblemished, youthful.

            Cancer and infection rot
            from inside out. Your organ
            donor card's a useless stub.

            I did not want to look
                at you. Contaminated
                      not even good for parts.

Kathy Engel

Dad, Pete and Obama

When Pete sang at the Lincoln Memorial I called to ash.
I had played Pete as your last breath slipped out,
the rest of you already gone.
Pete ushered you; your hero sang for the man
whose name you spoke the week you died:
Obama, you said, sipping water,
I believe something is happening, don't you?
Pete with his grandson who lived in Nicaragua,
the country we loved in its burning birth, Pete
who wouldn't testify, Pete Civil Rights, Pete Peace,
Pete 1199, Pete this land, our land—
Pete Clearwater, Pete and Toshi, Pete and
Brother Kirkpatrick, Pete and June reading poems
at the UN Rally circa 1983, Pete the unwavering
for all who were taken, all who picketed and as Pete said
for the young people who taught us not to be afraid
those Montgomery sit-in days, Pete in his power,
in the place of power, suspenders and banjo, train
chug of workers belting out a new old gusty day, ghosts
of resistance swaying past the monument, feeding
the hungry crowd, this day when Pete sang
at the Lincoln Memorial I called to you
who took a bus alone to D.C. at 80 to protest:
I called to your ash, Dad, who took me there first.

Anna M. Evans

Weltschmerz

I wasn't sure what I was going to find—
like padded cells or strait jackets, or worse—
the day my teenage daughter lost her mind.

The admin staff were gentle and resigned
to forms of loss. Like crashing in reverse,
I couldn't see what I'd once thought I'd find.

She'd said she felt unreal and then declined
to clarify. I wished I'd been a nurse
the day my teenage daughter lost her mind.

I smiled until my jaw ached as I signed
the papers, putting copies in my purse
I wasn't sure that I would ever find.

We waited for the therapist and dined
on crackers in a room safe as a hearse,
the day my teenage daughter lost her mind.

They told me she was suffering for mankind
and would get hardened to the universe—
a certain cure, but difficult to find
the day my teenage daughter lost her mind.

Meri Harary Fleischman

Remnants

Teacup warming your hands,
you delicately pinch its slim handle
curved like a child's arm resting on dainty hips.

A loud knock on the door of your Berlin flat
jolts you out of your favorite chair—
none of your neighbors knock so hard.
You open the door slowly, as if halting time.
A soldier stands outside, holding an urn,
red swastika bands his arm.

"Mrs. Wasserman? Fannie Wasserman?"
You answer, and he informs you
inside the urn are Freddy's remains—
ashes the remnants of your son,
taken from his flat and arrested,
missing for six weeks--
sent to Dachau concentration camp.
You wished they had allowed him
to take his coat.

The soldier demands 70 marks for the urn,
and you quickly pay, not knowing if it is
Freddy within the urn, or ashes of another,
but your reach for it,
this time capsule
holding thirty years of life--
cold and dull in your hands.
You close the door.
Holding the urn to your breast,
you place it on the kitchen table,
sit down, continue to drink your tea,
now cold and bitter.

Marisa Frasca

Pink Moon Child

Prendi, prendi fra le dita quella margherita che ti brucia il cuore...
"Take, take between your fingers that daisy which fuels the heart..."

It was the cloud of innocence and the tide rolled me out with white
music coming from the radio, mother singing, the sewing machine Necchi
churning like a train. We all shared a room. It was the bed where I lay
half awake, half walking in fields of tall stemmed daisies. I pulled tear
dropped white petals and I longed for her: *she loves me, loves me not.*

Daisies, little foot, Necchi's needle stopped. Mamma? What is that pink
zigzag on your lap? My new embroidered pillow? Tea napkin stitches?
Pink moon drops? Why does the machine sew pink sparks?
Pink is for my pink moon child. Stop asking; get your head out of the clouds.
I don't like pink pillows, dresses, pink anything or drinking from her glass.

Mezzogiorno—around the table eating I'm the only one without a glass.
Why? And why does Aldo have hair under his arms and not me? Looks
stop my swallowing. I shrink. Her heavy sigh, another sigh, hard blows of
breath bring stitched up tears. I know the moon is white, music, daisies over-

flow with questions. I tell myself next time try harder, next time try not to ask.

Celeste Gainey

In the late heat of August

Mrs. Kuskey, the saleslady from Magnin's,
drives out to the house in her Buick
and lays the dark, heavy dresses across my father's side of the
bed.

Nothing light and fine for a late summer funeral,
the store is already selling fall and winter fashions;
this is the best she can do.

The black horrifies, so Mom settles
on cocoa brown wool jersey,
belted, three-quarter length sleeves,

with a tiered hemline that would have stopped her
from buying the dress under normal circumstances.
My dad would have agreed, "No, that's not you. Too fussy,"

then, would have leaned back against the cool silk
of the faux Louis XVI settee in the Finer Fashions Salon,
waiting for her to reappear.

Roberto Carlos Garcia

Mama Ana's Regret

It happened on my birthday
so I'll always remember.
The phone rang
so early it could only be
a harbinger.
It woke me from a dream
where I stood on a crowded
sidewalk looking across
a six-lane highway
at another crowded sidewalk
& I attempted to cross
with my little cousin Josh.
Mama Ana's mother, her namesake,
screamed from the other side:
No, no cruzes!
& I grabbed Josh's arm.

A week or two later,
he'd be bitten by a Rottweiler.

I also woke to sobs.
Mama Ana had left
her mother's house
one week before she died.
& every year on my birthday
I remember her fret for us
& how she rushed away
from her mother for us
& how she sobbed,

Oh one more week.
One more.
Oh why?
Why?

Deborah Gerrish

Putting on Grief

I've put on grief—
know what it's like
to skip meals
lose memory
walk into walls

I've put on grief
as a hundred year old dress
hidden in a back closet

Borrowed from ancestors
my mother, aunts, grandmothers
great grandmothers

Torn with stains
a dreary faded gown
outlined in shadows
with dropped hem
and missing buttons

I've put on grief
a costume too large
for this invisible body
afraid its design
will unravel me
as tumbleweed

Wanting to move
on to another place
but not yet ready

to escape this
curse of sorrow

where with threadbare soul

I am sentenced to hollow
rooms to wait it out—

Gail Fishman Gerwin

A Pogrom Is a Pogrom

Aunt Rose
tells us about the times
Cossacks galloped through
Brest-Litovsk, slashed,
looted, terrified the little
children crouched next to
turnips and potatoes
in the root cellar.

Aunt Rose
tells us of her big white
house with red shutters,
a porch for tea with neighbors,
slatted fence around flowers,
perhaps tulips her father Jacob
planted when October winds
promised early snows for her,
tiny Sadie, brothers Ben and Morris.

Aunt Rose
tells us about the squalid steamer
that took her to America
with her mother Anna,
who'd waited in the East
until Jake could find a home
in Paterson, could find a job,
could send money for passage.

Aunt Rose,
now shrunken by the
bones in her back collapsing
one by one, sits on a tower
of pillows in her slow green Chevy.
Humbled by the deaths
of her husband, son, daughter.

Aunt Rose tells us again, again,
what the Cossacks missed,
cancer finished.

Sarah Ghoshal

Absence
(#2 for Rigs)

I am sure
they know
he's not here.

One of them,
nut-mouthed,
climbs over

slowly. Puts
hands to glass,
looks frantically,

scales the yell-
low can, makes
eye contact.

I knock. He
runs away,
satisfied.

There
is no
bark.

Yueh Goffin

Bound Feet

Twinkling two pointed breasts
her feet are bound
to push her waving round hips.
A snuff-bottled beauty
weak, tiny, and pale
she walks with a pickled smile
Making love
to a pair of
three-inch-lotus-petal toeless feet
men hold them so tight.

M.J. Iuppa

Fog rolled in late yesterday and stayed on, laying

low in the orchard with a wistfulness that refused
to burn in the break of May's brash sun. Instead
it brooded over its manuscript, memorizing
details soon to be lost in illumination...

                        Better to kiss lightly
these blades of grass, these new leaves that tear up
simultaneously– confirming its quick departure
as a loss counted without words.

Adele Kenny

Even Now
(For My Father)

Memory is easy here, in springtime's rimless light – and only a little rain to pattern the sky. There's a faint (perhaps remembered) scent of wild violet. Something sweet that stays. Shadows tumble through clouds. It's been more than thirty years – your death a grief that only now begins to know its name. All this time, I've rebuilt you out of dead leaves and wind, dumb with a feeling that even now, I can't express – as if that dark were your happiness and you ran to it, years too young to be dead, as if, even now, you might open your hand and reach through time to where I wait.

Patricia Kinney

Resurrection

Every day after work
he took my hand,
and we walked
through the cemetery
of cars in the backyard
to look at a classic
Harley sitting under tarp.
It took a year
'til he talked
of restoring:
*replace crushed
chrome, clean
bloody leather,
straighten bent
wheels, front forks,
add drag pipes,
saddlebags,
new gas tank*,
he listed one
night. His cheek gleamed
silver under a half
moon's light when he
knelt, stroked
the V-Twin
killed with his brother,
and I worried how
he'd grieve
when he brought old
steel back to life.

Alyse Knorr

After Jenny Asks Alice About Her Dead Sister

Shopping, let's go,
there are shrimp on sticks
at Delagio's and lipsticks
of every color and on the way,
there will be yellow tractors mowing
fields of sunflowers whose faces
have turned black.

Alyse Knorr

Alice in Georgialand

I named the mare O'Malley, saw her every day
on my drive to work, standing still as a pre-blitz
pool in a pasture at the corner of Post and Dickerson.
As a kid once made a Pegasus—cut a knight off
his steed and glued wings in his place. Rose took
it off my desk and carried the thing around with her
for months after, lisping those S's and galloping
the figure across our ice-laced windows and porch.
When my mother found it she shouted at me, said
I'd destroyed something perfectly new.

Judy Kronenfeld

After Her Headstone Is Placed on the First Anniversary of My Last Aunt's Death

There's an almost architectural darkness
I have inside—a blind-windowed edifice calling me
to feel my way around, mental hands searching
for the walls of wall-lessness,
mental eyes opening
to that darkness.

Near the dusty portal—as if shadowing
the scent of cold into the slow spacious
past—I pass my recent dead,
who seemingly might yet
turn and walk back into
sunshine; I mingle through them,
drinking in their absence,
and move further into the distances
of no distance, until there are places
of a different blackness.

And there I begin to lose
my outlines to the dark,
bristling toward me like the fur
of animals. I grow quiet
as a stopped clock,
and the darkness lightens
to the vaguest hologram
of dampened brightness on the inside
of my eyes.
And then I see
a glistening, faint as a frill
of oar foam across a river
black as sky—
the wet eyes

of my deepest dead, who dwell within
the thickening truth—
before the vista
and the edifice eclipse
like iris wipes
in a film, and I turn back,
flattened, into day.

Michelle Lerner

Pompeii

Sometimes daylight shines backward on your face
as if years
of brown floodwaters had not taken me whole
with your footprints downriver
washed me up on moraine
a different woman, mother,
canvass covered
with gouache
thick, thin, dull.
I don't know why I see you
in my dreams,
why I dream
why I
still sleep in that bed
on Commercial Ave
next to you
as in Pompeii
our outlines vivid in the petrified
ash
open-mouthed with longing.

Kristin Leskowits

Grandma, you were nothing like your mother

I discovered, long
after you let me fill up
shopping carts with toys,

when your hands ached as you tried
holding a needle to sew:

between four and five
you scaled the kitchen counter
to feed your brother.

You found empty cupboards; some
nights dog biscuits were dinner.

Your absent mother,
wrapped up in Broadway dreaming,
red rouge, cheap perfume,

returned home from auditions
long after you fell asleep.

Antoinette Libro

Our dear friend's death –
   her homemade soup still
      in the freezer

Charlotte Mandel

SEA CHANTEY

As a child I knelt
with cupped hands
to catch flickers of fish
transparent as the water
sounding   shush   shush
like memories of ancient prayer.

The morning surf spills ocherous foam.
Oil on a wave's twitching back
tars the feathers
of famished gulls
struggling to mount the wind.

Children run on our sands of denial
and slake thirsts
with numbing bubbles
bottled in plastic
the colors of jellyfish

cast like reliquary offerings
dutiful currents
ferry back to shore.

Yesenia Montilla

Scare

That morning
on the subway
when the fat man
caused me to gag
his skin smelling
of perspiration
something made with
curry, a dream dinner that
without his scent
would have been my
favorite plate of all time
I knew I was having
a baby

That night I dreamt of
diaperless babies
wrapped in poetry books
Butterfly's Burden — the
purple cover wrapped
between plump legs
sorrowful sobs
wanting eyes
a need

Morning again
I woke in sobs
leaned into my lover
cuddled into his stomach
acceptance maybe
then a cramp blistered under
like an eraser on old papyrus
It was the disappearance
of a life that would have been
could have been
magic

Vanishing like god's soft
beard against the world's satin
pillow, all of it
evaporating
with each
red
trickle

Pat Mottola

Aubergine

    - (aubergine, *n.* eggplant, indigenous to India, Burma, China and Vietnam)

I peel the thick outer layer
of aubergine skin, tough as your exterior,
dark as dried blood. I often cut myself
while trying to expose the soft flesh
beneath the surface. In Medieval times
it came with warnings: eggplant—
dark fruit, aphrodisiac to some.

Today there is silence.
Twenty years since you came back
from 'Nam, at home the fields are wet
as blood-soaked rice paddies.
After the rain I watch you
slog the slippery ground, planting crops
your first day home since you dried out
in rehab, again. Group therapy fails
to break your hardened skin.
Instead you keep your secrets,
bury your anger like seeds
sunk too deep within the earth.
You dig the fields like trenches
that protected you from Vietcong,
try to hide your wounds.

I fix dinner, slice through layers
of eggplant. Salt and rinse.
Still the pungent seeds locked inside.
While I savor soft, succulent meat,
you taste only bitterness,
and we both bleed.

Pat Mottola

The Wall

> *SP4 Edward Michael Tyszka*
> *February 28, 1948 - January 11, 1969*
> *Quang Tin, South Vietnam*

Alone, I search for my Cousin Eddie,
twenty. Families stand beside me looking
serious. I want to tell them he was voted
class clown his Senior year, would laugh
like a trickster who could twist
a nightmare back to light. I find him
inscribed in Panel 35W, Line 74,
trace his name, try to rub him out,

take him back home
to Aunt Betty. Instead I feel the chill
of polished granite, curse the slick
mass of stone that mocks my reflection.
It rains here every day. Under my umbrella
my face does not stay dry. I walk
the length of wall. Feet sink in mud
deep and foul as a Vietnamese jungle.

Megeen R. Mulholland

Crossing the Divide

He traveled by train
capturing each scene
in half frame--
noting exposure,
speed, and location,
en route to his final destination.

Each second here adds up to
only the present moment
as landscape stands
completely still through the viewfinder,
with "1/100 sec" written on back
as he records the details of his journey--
the idle stretch of grasses,
and the regular progression
of post and rails.

one onehundredth one onehundredth
"first hills of the Bitterroot range"
one onehundredth one onehundredth
"those rocks were amazing tints of pink and green"
one onehundredth one onehundredth one onehundredth
"Montana hills beginning to rise"
one onehundredth one onehundredth one onehundredth
"climbed several hours from the floor of the valley below"
one onehundredth one onehundredth one

In sequence the tracks ascend
into a rise of mountains
border by stationary border
until he reaches the peak,
too high and light to photograph
without risk of overexposure,
it remains invisible to me.

In the rest of his prints,
I follow his eventual descent,
each shot now quickly picking up the tracks
at a pace almost too rapid to capture
until we finally arrive
at the sudden flatlands
where the exhaled images fade,
save one crossed post rising
out of the final frame.

Megeen R. Mulholland

Foreshadowing

He must have seen
his darkened figure
in the foreground
of the photograph
looming large before him
as he looked through the viewfinder,
standing off to one side of the track.

The abandoned passenger car
is filled with darkened figures
and bystanders who peer
through its windows from the outside
as if at an exhibit;
they climb aboard and disembark,
some shrugging away from the train
with indifference to history.

I wish I could alight with them,
then surprise him
by turning toward the sun,
crossing the tracks,
and stepping into his shadow--
readjusting his focus
from this background
of black and white
to the tinge of color
foreshadowing our future.

Michelle Ovalle

Intervention

My muse holds me hostage
among painted skulls with flowers
for eyes, glitter teeth,
and the smell of freshly turned soil –
the dead have made this dirt a dance floor.

Lulu expects too much, refusing to give
back my shatter, wanting me to wrap my mouth
around skulls and spit out eternities.
I can't write unless there's a crack.

She walks up to me, hips swaying effortlessly,
grabs my shirt collar and whispers,

Girl, I ain't lettin' you go 'till you learn to kiss the dead.

Linda Radice

For My Brother

I met you long before infant safety seats,
your tiny face over our mother's shoulder,

and you refused to answer me on that ride
from the hospital, despite my repeated self-

introductions as your big sister. I walked
a step behind as you - still silent - my only

sibling - was carried through the door and
into the house. The four years between us

made me the protector, you the little brat
who teased without mercy, but whose fists

flew at John Johnstone one summer afternoon
when he threw dirt in my face and called me

"fatso." It seemed so natural to finish your
sentences fifty years later when the tumor

invaded your brain, stole some words, but left
your sense of humor intact. We laughed at the

memory of Dad - a bowl of spaghetti turned over
his head by our young spitfire mother. The table

next to your chair was full of chocolates, the
doctor ordered you to eat your fill. I didn't tell

you that I always knew who swiped the Hershey
bars from my Halloween candy. At the end,

we fed you chocolate ice cream and morphine,
turned you every half hour, counted your breaths.

I talked to you –you couldn't answer.
You died in the house we grew up in,
I stood by the door when they carried you out.

Mina Santomenno

Going, going

The table is set for strangers.
I notice he included the tiny crow
We bought on our honeymoon
When everything was beautiful and precious.
I watch him laugh with the new neighbor,
Her pretty smile demur,
While on the white surface,
Everything is for sale.

Heidi Sheridan

Awash

My lover says spirits know when
to return and go into this world.
We are not in control of the rocks.

First one felt like a bad period.
Second an induced mini labor.
This one, not mine.
Third, a hope passing, like
grace waving as it flew with a red hawk.

Calcium, placenta, tissue,
and bone go through pipes,
sewage treatment plants.

They meet in rivers or oceans
to bemoan their diluted luck.
I cull their echoes as I swim.

Lisa Sisler

Full Circle

We found out about Agnes on Friday night
We had come home from the day's adventures—
mall trips, pick-up football games at the Cornfields,
an extra day's work at the Candy Store in town—
It had been an artificial holiday, teachers' convention,
a four-day weekend with plans of sleep and parties,
sneaking bottles from cabinets to the sanctity
of our hands, our lips, the circles we stood in for the pass.

We got the phone call.
Plans canceled.
Bottles remained on the shelf.

While we were at the movies, making out
in backseats with our boyfriends, warring
with our mothers, watching the kid
on *Beverly Hills 90210* accidentally shoot himself

Agnes woke up that morning, planning her death
the way we planned a party, with fear and acceleration.

Or if her act was a frustrated burst of fuck-it, rash and teenage,
the circle of childhood friends we were,
standing in a driveway that Friday night,
kicking asphalt, avoiding each other's eyes,
never did figure it out.

Odarka Polanskyj Stockert

I am burning sage

on this cold morning
and the house will not warm
the stove is devouring
the last of the winter's wood
and the sage I cut last week
preparing for spring's new growth
it has dried brittle.

It catches fire quickly and evenly
glowing along the edges
and slowing
as the burn reaches the stems that are thicker
I lay the smoking ember
on the stove top to scent the air
to smoke away the darkness
the dank winter shadow
that drains the psyche
to absorb the negatively inclined
I will purge
I will breath the smoky air
I will blow the ash in circles
it will land at my feet.

I walk the glow twig to the doorway
where things linger
I walk it to the room upstairs
where anger is stuck
and leave the cinder in a bowl
to smoke vanity from the mirror
jealousy from winter coat that everyone admires
and regret from the torn shearling, delicate with age
tearing at the patched repair
later I will move to the other rooms
each in its own turn
will be smoked and drained of darkness

sad ideas, energies undirected
(who knows where they may end)
and prying eyes
the things devouring the deep insides.

I burn sage in sorrow
sorrow burns the sage
until tomorrow burn,
fires hot and smoky
burn undissipated rage!

Anique Taylor

Mourning in the Days of Joy
The Last Day of Sukkoth
Nineteen Days Since You Died

On the final day
of Judgment as the New
Year is set, I tighten my quilted
shroud around me, sink into the tired
couch as far away families celebrate in
breakable houses of two-and-a half walls; fronds
to see through to the stars; who pray with the spine of
palm, two mouths of willow, three eyes of myrtle, a heart of
citron; those who

dip bread in honey.
I pour green tea from a
thrift store carafe as they circle
seven times, carrying bundles of five
willows to strike the ground five times. They
shake loose the leaves as it is decided who will be
judged and how the rain with fall as dark matter begins
to form in elongated

wisps and the vanishing
point of my life fails like a
distant star (the fragility of human
shelter) on the gray couch. Watching TV
reruns, stationary as the world continues to circle
without you. The commandment of joy broken, I close my
eyes to hide my sin of weeping.

Madeline Tiger

ON CRETE   1980
in memory of Homer Martin Tiger Bass, 1967-1989

Homer told me in an excited voice that this castle, Kronos,
where we were strolling, would have been a terrific place for a
kid to live:
he could have wandered all around these corridors, playing hide-
and-seek

There were mosaics on the walls, faded pastels, lovely figures—
men and women or boys and girls. I was standing in front of one
for a long time. Homer had wandered around a sort of corner
to another "chamber". I said the word ios, paused and smiled
toward where he had taken off, testing adventure.

He was about to enter the Labyrinth. I followed, of course, and
lost track
We wandered for I don't know how much time. We called out to
each other,
echoing. We knew the story of the Minotaur. Maybe our voices
became
our threads, in and out of walled-in alleys, around and around.
Homer wasn't as nervous as I was, now I remember
hearing him laugh. On the edge of adolescence, he was coming
into
a deep, hearty laugh. Much taller than I, he was a figure of
slender height
like a beautiful young man, in profile, on one of those walls.

I barely remember him as a child
except in dreams. In dreams I'm always saving him —
from trains, from a platform, left behind the rest of the family,
from being on a sled or a stretcher
going into the distance, but never saving him from the sea.
I never dream about the Tasmanian Sea.
I never dream about those bays between the islands (I forget
their names)

or about his kayak. He took a picture of himself, in a yoga pose, smiling wide
beside his kayak…

I never dreamed about Crete or the Labyrinth,
but it was always there—I know now—underneath my dreams.
When we were getting lost in the Labyrinth, Homer was laughing.
I was nervous and proud of how my son could find his way—

I have to stop here, so I won't have to write
the dire part — so I can leave with our hitch-hiking adventures on Crete,
learning thalassa ble, the blue sea, saying ios, Homerus, knowing
the blue shining of Homer's eyes.

Laura Whalen

Isla De Ons, 2007

We walked like pilgrims, footsore
on the paths around the blue island
coming to ~~the~~ *el agujero del infierno,*

where waves tossed the cliffs below—
the place where the Galician Celts
listened for the voices of their dead.

You and I, we heard nothing then.
It would not be until years later when
returning our dear dead would sing to us:

Not sad songs but those of deepest
longing for our breathing lives,
the cups of wine and hot coffee,

the green of our gardens—
songs for children suddenly grown,
songs for the world they have left

with us to hold gently in our reddened hands
so like the precious fragments of shell
on the shore below to treasure, as best we can.

Laura Winters

There Will Your Heart Be Also

Last night I had a dream about virtual reality
a glove and wind and a huge dome
onto which was projected
what I have longed for every night since my grandmother died
twenty-eight years ago
not just combing her soft hair
not just touching her hard hands
but being in the place in which I knew her
the four-block area on Route 46
a blur people pass at sixty miles an hour
That's what I called home
The sidewalk from Fountains of Wayne
to Dover Furniture
to The Anthony Wayne Char Broil Hamburgers and Hotdogs
The walk to Two Guys to get Pall Malls and rye bread
I'd warn her of every hole
"Not there, Nonny. Come this way."
But she died anyway
no matter how much warning I gave
and now I see her in my dreams
Last night I knew I wasn't really flying over the place I miss
not actually on the verge of seeing her
but I was there through virtual reality
not to do something I'd only dreamed of
but to get back something that never should have gone
reality itself now virtual enough without her

ESSAYS

From the guest editor...

> "...Sick of fear I eat and preen, whisper to my dead who made me when they were young and taught me to keep a wish even a mini-vision going under the drum-tight clock tower."
>
> from "When on a Late March Evening" in **The Water Books**, by Judith Vollmer

When Christine invited me to guest edit a special issue of her beloved journal, I was excited at the prospect to work with and learn from her and with the poets and artists who would be sending us their work. When she told me the edition would be a collection of poems and essays on how women grieve, I felt as if I were handed a great gift.

Between the years of 1997 and 2003, I lost most of the generation before mine. My mother, first, at 51 years old, and my father last, at 63 years old. In between them, were the deaths of three grandparents, two uncles, and aunt, a sister-in-law and brother-in-law. This list does not include dear friends or their family members, or distant relatives. All of this beginning when I was 34 years old, raising two children, ages 12 and 15, working full time, attending college part time, active in various communities. Some of my dear ones needed constant care in the months and even years leading up to their deaths. For others, it was sudden. Either way, it was *always* a shock, another empty hole opening in both my body and in the universe, forcing me to find a new way to survive, to keep the faith, to be a person of hope, to be actively present to the people I love who were also trying, through their own grieving, to navigate this new world.

The thought that people who didn't know me before each loss might not know me fully -- because I was changed so each time, because a piece of me was missing, because the universe was very different -- was immediately central to me after my mother's death. It remains important today, yet giving myself over fully to the deep and wide reading and writing of poetry has provided a true and intimate place to explore metaphors and images and sounds of loss. Poetry asks the questions and provides glimmers of understanding, of resiliency, of mercy and hope and charity as we consider the many and varied reasons and ways we grieve. The poet, essayist, and funeral director, Thomas Lynch wrote in an essay entitled, *Good Grief: An Undertaker's Reflections,*

> "And grief, good grief... is something about which we have little choice. It is the tax we pay on the loves of our lives, our habits and attachments. And like every other tax there is this dull math to it -- if you love, you grieve. So the question is not so much whether or not, but rather how well, how completely, how meaningfully we mourn..."

Poetry speaks to how meaningfully we mourn. And, poetry moves us from the deeply personal to the communal, from our own way of facing it (or not) to exploring the ways and reasons our own grief experiences bring light and, perhaps, a shred of wisdom to the conversation. As Gregory Orr explains in <u>Poetry as Survival</u>:

> " But in the act of making a poem at least two crucial things have taken place that are different from ordinary life. First, we have shifted the crisis to a bearable distance from us: removed it to the symbolic but vivid work of language. Second, we have actively made and shaped this model for our situation rather than passively endured it as a lived experience."

Adanna Literary Journal seeks to share the art of women and men who reflect on the topics, ideas, and experiences that are central for women. Facing grief and finding a way to survive it certainly fits its mission. We are glad that two men, one poet and one visual artist, submitted work that we are pleased to include in the conversation. Whether one believes that women and men grieve differently or similarly, we do know that our lived experiences do influence one another. And, at least most women I have talked with or read, appreciate the terrible beauty of this expression through the art of a man in the same, and sometimes more powerfully moving, way we do through the art of a woman. In her poem "In Blackwater Woods," Mary Oliver wrote:

> To live in this world
>
> you must be able
> to do three things:
> to love what is mortal;
> to hold it
>
> against your bones knowing
> your own life depends on it;
> and, when the time comes to let it go,
> to let it go.

This is a hard-learned gift of wisdom that transcends all boundaries, and speaks to all human beings.

    When we began this project, Christine and I had agreed on including 30 poems. As we read and re-read the hundreds of submitted poems, we kept saying to each other, "Just one more?" This collection of poems represents poets who are published for their first time through poets who have published several collections. It includes poems that invite us to consider women's experiences of grieving the deaths and/or losses of parents, children, friends, lovers, pets, relationships, and of the natural world, and spiritual or political faith. Some poets are writing about losses more recent and close to home, while others are writing about losses that span generations and the continents. Each poem stands alone and then adds something unique to the collection, and in both ways, they ask our readers to explore the questions that transform us, that help us make meaning of our tragedies. As these poems come together here to create a body, they heighten our awareness of how we actually live in our own physical bodies and as one body in a community finding its way to survive loss.

Of course I have suffered losses before and after 1997-2003, and as long as I am living, I know I am not finished. I offer you here two of my own attempts to figure out at least a little something about the experience of grief:

she comes to me in lilacs

it isn't enough to inhale her fragrance
in the first spring blooming

or to search for her in each significant bud

i find her under my naked feet
in sleepy winter roots

she whispers under my naked feet

i have not abandoned you

cutting a bagel as my father lay dying

turn the blade away from yourself
was his fierce final warning
you can hardly anticipate
edge severing edge
six layers
deep

I hope all of the poems and essays and artwork of this "How Women Grieve" edition of *Adanna* will invite you to explore the question Mary Oliver asks in another poem, "Stars": What can we do / but keep on breathing in and out, / modest and willing, and in our places?

Lynne McEniry

The House of Grief: Writing About Loss

"However, in pursuing the impossible, I did learn something. Each of us is so ashamed of his own helplessness and ignorance that he considers it appropriate to communicate only what he thinks others will understand. There are, however, times when somehow we slowly divest ourselves of that shame and begin to speak openly about things we do not understand."
Czeslaw Milosz, <u>To Begin Where I Am</u>

My students sometimes ask me why all of the poems we read together are so sad. Granted, I teach modernist and postmodern literature, and if a reader is to love writing from the last hundred years, as I do, she must be willing to find profound beauty in brokenness, and she must wish to explore how to survive (and thrive) after the worst has happened. I tell my students that literature is complex because our inner and our outer lives are complex, that poems can be mysterious because our motives and our behaviors are often mysterious.

We tend not to need explanations or justifications for happiness and joy. They are, in and of themselves, complete and whole. We do, however, need to understand our sorrows and our griefs, and poets are at the forefront of the attempt to find a new and often estranging language for the life-alerting experiences of loss and death. Each poem about death, whether written from the trenches in the immediate aftermath of loss or "recollected in tranquility" years afterward, attempts to pay tribute and bear witness to the process that Thomas Attig calls "relearning the world."

In <u>The Year of Magical Thinking</u>, Joan Dideon writes, "Grief turns out to be a place none of us knows until we reach it." Having worked for more than a decade with grief and bereavement groups, I agree with Dideon. Each house of grief is unique and individual. Its rooms and corridors can be frightening and unsettling, its windows and doors either locked up tight or thrown wide open to the world. And don't get me started on the basement. Oh, the basement can be so psychologically disorienting that some never come back up the stairs. But poets, in some ways, willingly enter the house of grief and take a courageous look around. In <u>The Redress of Poetry</u>, Seamus Heaney writes, "if our given experience is a labyrinth, then its impassibility is countered by the poet's imagining some equivalent of the labyrinth and bringing himself and the reader through it." I don't know a labyrinth more treacherous than loss, and I admire the poets in and out of this volume who are willing to enter the house of grief and lead us in, through, and beyond it.

Laura Winters

BIOGRAPHICAL NOTES

Jasmine Araujo, from Red Hook, NY, is a senior at Bard College where she has studied under poets including Celia Bland, Michael Ives, and most recently Robert Kelly.

Cara Armstrong is a Visiting Professor in the School of Architecture and Art at Norwich University as well as a student in the Drew University MFA in Poetry program.

Wendy Barnes is a graduate of the MFA program in Writing at California Institute of the Arts and a doctoral student in the Arts and Letters Program at Drew University. Her poems have appeared *Faultline, Spiral Orb*, *Painted Bride Quarterly* and other journals. Wendy's chapbook, *So-Called Mettle*, was published early this year (Finishing Line Press).

Elliott batTzedek earned an MFA in Poetry in Translation from Drew University, for which she is translating poems by the Israeli Jewish lesbian writer Shez. She works as a literacy consultant, as staff in an independent bookstore, as adjunct graduate school faculty, and as co-leader of Fringes, a poetry-based havurah. Her work appears in *Two Lines Translation Anthology, Overplay/Underdone: Poems in the Third Dimension, Adanna Contemporary Love Poems, Armchair/Shotgun, Poetica, Poemeleon, Trivia, Naugatuck River Review, Lamba Literary Online, Sinister Wisdom,* and as a Split This Rock poem of the week.

Christine Beck, a retired professor of legal studies, will receive an MFA in Poetry degree from Southern Connecticut State University in 2013. Her chapbook, *Sometimes He Comes Home Bloody*, is forthcoming from Pudding House Press. She is the President of the Greater New Haven Chapter of the Connecticut Poetry Society.

Mary Brancaccio is studying for her MFA in Poetry at Drew University. She was a finalist in the 2012 narrative poetry contest in *Nagatuck River Review*. Her poetry has appeared in *Chantarelle's Notebook, Lake Affect Magazine* and *Chest* journal. One of her poems has been included in a Japanese anthology of poems written in response to the earthquake and tsunami that struck Japan in March 2011. She also has poems in the *Edison Literary Review*. Brancaccio was recently appointed an assistant professor at the Caspersen School of Graduate Studies at Drew University. She taught creative writing in Maplewood, New Jersey for many years.

Elizabeth Catanese is an artist, poet, and art history teacher who lives and works in suburban Philadelphia. Her paintings and art installations have been exhibited in the juried Dangerous Women II exhibition at Mercer County Community College and at Bryn Mawr College. She won Bryn Mawr College's Academy of American Poets prize in 2006 and was a finalist for Calyx's Lois Cranston Memorial Prize in 2009.

Luisa Caycedo-Kimura was born in Colombia and grew up in New York City. She has received awards for her poetry and was recently nominated for The Pushcart Prize. Her poems appear or are forthcoming in *San Pedro River Review*, *Connecticut Review*, *Ellipsis... Literature and Art*, *PALABRA*, *Sunken Garden Poetry 1992-2011*, and others.

Lucia Cherciu is a Professor of English at SUNY / Dutchess in Poughkeepsie, NY, and her poetry appeared in *Connecticut Review, Cortland Review, Memoir (and), Legacies, Spillway,* and other literary magazines, both in English and in Romanian. Her books of poetry are "Lepădarea de Limbă" (Editura Vinea, 2009), and "Altoiul Râsului" (Editura Brumar, 2010).

David Crews (davidcrewspoetry.com) has poems published or forthcoming in The Greensboro Review, The Southeast Review, The Carolina Quarterly, Berkeley Poetry Review, Paterson Literary Review, Tar River Poetry, and others. Essays found in Adanna Literary Journal and SPECTRUM. Most recently, he has been nominated for a Pushcart Prize.

Barbara Crooker was a recent finalist for the 2011 NJ Poet's Prize. Her books are *Radiance*, which was a finalist for the 2006 Paterson Poetry Prize; *Line Dance*, (Word Press 2008), which won the 2009 Paterson Award for Literary Excellence; and *More* (C & R Press, 2010). Her poems also appear in: *Good Poems American Places* and the *Bedford Introduction to Literature*.

Jessica de Koninck, a long time resident of Montclair, NJ, has a B.A. from Brandeis, a J.D. from Boston University and MFA from Stonecoast. She is the author of the collection *Repairs*, and her poems appear in *The Valparaiso Poetry Review, The Paterson Literary Review, U.S. 1 Worksheets, Adanna Literary Journal* and elsewhere.

Kathy Engel has worked at the juncture of social justice and art for more than 30 years. She was a 2012 Split This Rock Featured Poet; her work is most recently in The Mom Egg and The Beloit Poetry Journal/Split This Rock 2012 Chapbook. She teaches in Art and Public Policy at NYU and co directs, with Alexis De Veaux, Lyrical Democracies.

Anna M. Evans' poems have appeared or are forthcoming in the *Harvard Review*, *Atlanta Review*, *Rattle*, *American Arts Quarterly*, and *32 Poems*. She gained her MFA from Bennington College, and is the Editor of the *Raintown Review*. Recipient of a 2011 Fellowship from the MacDowell Artists' Colony, she currently teaches at West Windsor Art Center and Richard Stockton College of NJ. Her chapbooks *Swimming* and *Selected Sonnets* are available from Maverick Duck Press. Visit her online at www.annamevans.com.

Meri Harary Fleischman lives in Hamden, CT with her husband and four children. She is a student in Southern Connecticut University's MFA program. She recently completed a chapbook of Holocaust poems, and is the 2112 winner of the Leo Connellan Poetry Prize from the Connecticut University System. Her winning poem will be published in the *Connecticut Review*.

Marisa Frasca's poems and translations have been published in *Voices Italian Americana, Philadelphia Poets, Arba Sicula, Poetry in Performance, Feile-Festa* and *Sweet Lemons II*. She has given bi-lingual readings at The Bowery Poetry Club, Cornelia Street Café, Hofstra U., St. Johns U., and City College. Frasca is a board member of The Italian American Writers Association, and is currently attending Drew's MFA program in Poetry and Poetry in Translation. Born in Vittoria, Italy, she resides in Manhasset, NY.

Celeste Gainey has had a long career as a lighting designer for both film and architecture. She is a 2010 graduate of Carlow University's MFA program. Her chapbook, *In the land of speculation & seismography,* a runner-up for the 2010 Robin Becker Chapbook Prize was published by Seven Kitchens Press in their 2011 Summer Kitchen Series.

Roberto Carlos Garcia's work has appeared in the *Istanbul Literary Review*, *Poets & Artists Magazine*, *Metazen* and *The New Gnus Literary Review*. Roberto is a member of the online writers community Fictionaut. A native New Yorker, he now lives and works in NJ where he is pursuing an MFA in Poetry and Poetry Translation at Drew University. Follow Roberto Carlos Garcia on Twitter at @thespokenmind.

Deborah Gerrish is an award winning poet whose poems have appeared in *The Paterson Literary Review*, *Lips*, *Ararat*, *Exit 13*, *Goldfinch*, and various anthologies. She was "Poet in Residence" at the Presbyterian Church of New Providence, NJ (2005–2008) and a featured poet on Breathearts.org. Her chapbook, *The Language of Rain,* was published in 2008; forthcoming is her collection of poems, *The Language of Paisley*. She has taught in NJ for over thirty years as a high school English teacher.

Gail Fishman Gerwin's poetry, book reviews, essays, and plays appear in journals and other outlets. She is associate poetry editor of *Tiferet*. Her memoir *Sugar and Sand* was a 2010 Paterson Poetry Prize finalist and her poems earned four consecutive Allen Ginsberg Poetry Awards honorable mentions. She owns *inedit*, a Morristown, NJ, writing/editing firm. She and her husband, Kenneth have two daughters, three grandsons, and a granddaughter.

Sarah Ghoshal is a writer and poet from Central NJ. She has had work published in several literary such as *Downtown Brooklyn, Brooklyn Paramount, Press 1* and *Edison Literary Review*. A writing professor at Montclair State University, she is active in the academic community and recently had her first short memoir, *My Suburbia*, published as an e-book on Amazon.

Yueh Henny Goffin was born in China and later moved to Taiwan. Poetry is her first love, and she considers every person's life a long poem that reveals itself gradually to delight God and people. Yueh now lives in NJ and is the author of "Rivers of Living Water - A Visual Harmony of the Four Gospels."

M.J. Iuppa lives on a small farm near the shores of Lake Ontario. Her most recent poems have appeared in Poetry East, The Chariton Review, Tar River Poetry, Blueline, The Prose Poem Project, and The Centrifugal Eye, among others. Recent chapbook is As the Crows Flies (Foothills Publishing, 2008) and second full length collection, Within Reach, (Cherry Grove Collections, 2010). She is Writer-in-Residence and Director of the Visual and Performing Arts Minor program at St. John Fisher College, Rochester, NY.

Adele Kenny is the author of 23 books (poetry and nonfiction). Her poems have been published in journals worldwide, as well as in books and anthologies published by Crown, McGraw-Hill, Tuttle, and Shambhala. A former creative writing professor at the College of New Rochelle, she is founding director of the Carriage House Poetry Series and poetry editor of Tiferet.

Patricia Kinney received her BA in Communications from Keystone College, and will be attending SUNY Binghamton in the fall for an MA in English. Her poetry is inspired by the people that she loves. Her work has appeared or is forthcoming in *Indigo Rising, Yes Poetry, WritingRaw.com*, and *Word Fountain*. She lives in rural PA.

Alyse Knorr received my MFA from George Mason University, where she served as poetry editor of *So to Speak: A Feminist*

Journal of Language and Art. Her work has appeared or is forthcoming in *RHINO, Sentence, Puerto Del Sol, Salamander, Cold Mountain Review, The Minnesota Review,* and others. In the summer of 2012, she will complete a residency at the Vermont Studio Center and read in the Joaquin Miller Poetry Series.

Judy Kronenfeld's most recent book of poems is *Shimmer* (WordTech Editions, 2012). *Light Lowering in Diminished Sevenths*, winner of the Litchfield Review Poetry Book Prize for 2007, has been re-issued in a revised second edition (Antrim House, 2012). Her poems have appeared in many print and online magazines including *Cimarron Review, Natural Bridge,* and *Calyx*, as well as in a dozen anthologies--most recently, *Before We Have Nowhere to Stand Israel Palestine: Poets Respond to the Struggle* (Lost Horse Press, 2012).

Michelle Lerner is an attorney, poet, mother, and cat rescuer living in NJ. She holds an MFA from the New School and her poems have been published in numerous journals and anthologies.

Kristin Leskowits lives in NJ and is a June 2012 graduate of the Drew University MFA in Poetry program. She has a BA in English and Fine Arts, a minor in Writing, and a MA in Teaching, all from Drew. She hopes to find a full time teaching position in the fall while writing and publishing poems, painting, and tutoring.

Antoinette Libro was awarded Third Place in the 2011 Allen Ginsberg Poetry Contest; in 2008 she received an Editor's Choice in the same contest. She publishes short form poetry; her tanka will be included in Take Five: Best Contemporary Tanka Anthology for 2011, published by Keibooks. Her work most recently appeared in red lights, moon bathing, Adanna Literary Journal Love Poems, and the Atlas Poetica Special Feature on Botanical Tanka, From Lime Trees to Eucalypts, online.

Charlotte Mandel is the winner of the 2012 New Jersey Poets Prize. She has published seven books of poetry, the most recent ROCK VEIN SKY from Midmarch Arts Press. Previous titles include two poem-novellas of feminist biblical revision, THE LIFE OF MARY and THE MARRIAGES OF JACOB.

Lynne McEniry is a poet with work published in Adanna, 5 A.M., The Stillwater Review, and Paterson Literary Review. She won Honorable Mention in the 2011 Allen Ginsberg Poetry Awards and collaborates on a variety of readings and workshops, including those in conversation with visual arts at the Maloney Art Gallery and Visual Arts Center of NJ. She holds an MFA in Poetry from Drew University and works at the College of Saint Elizabeth in Morristown, NJ.

Yesenia Montilla is a New York City poet with Cuban and Dominican roots. She earned her MFA in Poetry and Poetry in Translation from Drew University. She is one of the co-founders of Poets for Ayiti, her poetry has appeared in the chapbook "For The Crowns of Your Heads."

Pat Mottola received an M.S. in Art Education and an M.F.A. in Creative Writing from Southern Connecticut State University, where she currently teaches writing. Her work is published in numerous journals including *War, Literature & the Arts, Connecticut Review, Main Street Rag, San Pedro River Review,* and *Welter.* She was awarded the Leslie Leeds Poetry Prize, the Leo Connellan award, and the John Holmes Award. Pat is editor of *Connecticut River Review.*

Megeen R. Mulholland lost her father when she was six-months old and has explored her family's photographs ever since. She earned her Ph.D. from the University at Albany where she served as a managing editor of *13th Moon: A Feminist Literary Magazine.* She is also a graduate of the MA program in English and Creative Writing at SUNY, Binghamton. Her work has been accepted for publication in numerous anthologies and literary journals, and she is currently an assistant professor of English at

Hudson Valley Community College, where she teaches writing and co-edits the on-line journalism magazine *Faces*.

Michelle Ovalle is a NJ poet who graduated with an MFA from Drew University. Her work has appeared in the *Edison Literary Review* and is forthcoming in the anthology titled *Dear Sister*. When not writing poetry, Michelle enjoys photography, mosh pits, and red dresses.

Linda Radice is a poet and essayist. Her work has been published in numerous journals and anthologies. She was the second place recipient of the 2007 Allen Ginsberg Award. She is an active reader in a variety of venues and recently read with Pulitzer Prize winner Philip Schultz. She has two children and a granddaughter, and lives in North Plainfield, NJ with her husband Sam and a cat named Sonnet.

Christine Redman-Waldeyer, founder of *Adanna*, has been published in Caduceus, Lips, Motif Magazine, Paterson Literary Review, Seventh Quarry, Schuylkill Valley Journal, The Texas Review, Verse Wisconsin, among others. She has twice finaled in the Allen Ginsberg Poetry Awards. Book publications include: Frame by Frame, Gravel, and Eve Asks, Muse-Pie Press. She holds a doctorate in letters with a concentration in writing from Drew University.

Mina Santomenno is married and has a daughter, son and granddaughter. She is a former cloistered nun of the Dominican Monastery of Our Lady of the Perpetual Rosary and a graduate of Trinity College in Hartford, CT with a BS in Psychology. She is a member of the Connecticut Poetry Society.

Heidi Sheridan is from California and lives in NJ. Her poems have appeared in literary journals such as *ABZ Press, Carpenter Gothic Press, Shaking Like A Mountain, Amoebas,* and *Sophie's Wind*. Educated at the University of California Riverside and Cal Poly San Luis Obispo, she currently teaches Creative Writing and English at Ocean County College. She is pursuing an MFA in Poetry at Drew University.

Lisa Sisler is the editor of *Knocking at the Door: Approaching the Other*, a poetry anthology from Birch Bench Press, an imprint of Write Bloody Books, and is the assistant editor of *OVS* magazine and *Trio House Press*. Her work has appeared in *Contemporary American Voices* and *Connotation Press*, among others.

Odarka Polanskyj Stockert is a NJ native poet and long time member of South Mountain Poets and the Yara Arts Group. Odarka is a harpist and songwriter, an engineer and inventor. She lives in Millburn, with her family. Visit her at: http://www.facebook.com/pages/Odarkas-Poetry-Page/250392821524. Odarka's poetry has been previously published in a variety of journals.

Anique Taylor has read her poetry at some of Manhattan's hottest poetry venues: The St. Mark's Poetry Project, Dixon Place, The Speakeasy, ABC No Rio, Charas, and the Bowery Poetry Club. She is published in The World, Cheap Review, Big Fish, The National Poetry Magazine of the Lower East Side, and Cover Magazine. She is an MFA candidate in Poetry at Drew University.

Maurice Thomassen is a professional artist in the discipline of collage painting. A native of the Netherlands, he received his received his MFA at the Jan van Eyck Academy. He immigrated to the US in 2009. His work can be found in international private, corporate, and museum collections.

Madeline Tiger's most recent collections of poems are Birds of Sorrow and Joy: New and Selected Poems, 1970-2000 (2003), The Earth Which Is All (2008), The Atheist's Prayer (2010), and From the Viewing Stand (2011). She has been teaching poetry writing since 1973 and has been a "Dodge Poet" since 1986. She has five children and seven grandchildren and lives in Bloomfield under a weeping cherry tree.

Laura Whalen is a writer/editor living in Albany, New York. She has studied at the New York State Writer's Institute and The

Vermont Studio Center. She enjoys travel to the Adirondacks and the regions of Spain and Colombia. Her work has appeared in *Adanna*'s inaugural issue, *Blueline* and *Sugar Mule*.

Laura Winters is professor of English at the College of Saint Elizabeth, where she has taught literature, writing, and film for 30 years. For 20 years, she has been teaching in the graduate school at Drew University, where she was named Professor of the Year at the 2012 Commencement ceremony. She has recently used poetry as prompts for bearing witness and paying tribute in writing workshops for bereavement groups for families of firefighters lost in the line of duty, families of suicides, and families who lost loved ones on 9/11.